How The Railway Bridge

A Victorian Magic Lantern Show

The Forth Railway Bridge is a world-famous landmark just north of Edinburgh in Scotland. It has carried trains across the Firth of Forth since 1890 and still has the power to make those who travel over it or who stand on the shore to view it, gasp in admiration at its grandeur and the skills of the Victorian engineers and workmen who built it, over fifty of whom died doing so.

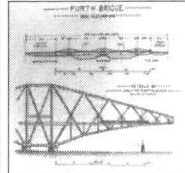

This book reproduces thirty-two Victorian magic lantern slides and the lecturer's scripts that accompanied them at the time they were published.

The Magic Lantern

The magic lantern was the predecessor of the pre-digital slide projector. The first magic lanterns were made in the mid-1600s by natural philosophers, (early scientists) who were exploring the nature and commercial potential of optics. Light sources and lenses improved throughout the 1700s and 1800s and, as a consequence, it was possible to show bigger, brighter and clearer pictures to ever larger audiences. During Queen Victoria's reign, magic lantern shows became established as mass-media entertainment. Shows could be lavish, theatrical events with all the razzmatazz of today's TV talent contests, with multiple lanterns to produce special effects. Magic lanterns were also used in Church and village halls and educational establishments for talks and lectures and, of course, in ordinary homes for family entertainment.

Some slides gave the illusion of movement. These included colourful kaleidoscopes, children skipping, a dentist pulling teeth and a man swallowing rats as he sleeps with his mouth open …… still a favourite with children (of all ages) who attend my magic lantern shows.

In the early 1800s, magic lanterns were used to create phantasmagoria horror shows, where terrifying devils, witches and the grim reaper were conjured out of thin air, with accompanying sound effects, in suitably scary venues. These shows employed the latest technology and created sophisticated illusions to entice customers to part with their money and be scared out of their wits.

Magic lantern slides were made of glass. Early ones were hand painted and expensive to produce and buy but, from the mid-1800s, photographic images were applied to slides, mass-production followed and the magic lantern industry boomed. In its heyday, the 1890s, countless millions of slides were produced, particularly in Britain, France and America, for entertainment, amusement, education, spiritual enlightenment and moral crusades.

Many sets of photographic 'lecture' slides were published on a very wide range of subjects but few have survived complete and with their accompanying notes.

The Forth Railway Bridge slides

Two Victorian, Scottish, photograph publishing businesses (founded by George Washington Wilson and James Valentine) took photographs of the construction of the bridge from its start in 1882 to the opening ceremony in 1890. Both created a set of magic lantern slides with a 'reading' (script), which could be purchased or hired by professional and amateur lantern lecturers, to educate and entertain audiences. The photographs and text in this book are reproduced from original slides and readings in my collection. I have included Wilson's and Valentine's readings as, whilst they tell the same story, in many respects they complement rather than duplicate each other and the wealth of information they contain justifies the inclusion of both.

The scripts contain fascinating historical background, anecdotes, facts, figures and technical details and the images are a testament to Britain's Victorian photographers and to one of the greatest engineering achievements of the period.

I hope you this enjoy this armchair tour of the construction of the Forth Railway Bridge.

Andrew Gill

The Valentine Slides

How the Forth Bridge was Built

The deep interest shown by all classes in the progress of the Forth Bridge shows that it may be considered a national achievement of engineering skill. When it was first proposed to connect the north and south shores of the Firth of Forth by a viaduct, the immense difficulties in the way of such an undertaking were looked upon as insuperable. The distance was not nearly so great as in the case of the Tay Bridge but the channel of the Forth was here 200 feet deep, and communication by the river could not be interrupted. The height of the bridge had necessarily to be very much greater than that of the Tay Bridge. The contractors, Messrs. Fowler and Baker, proposed a bridge on the new principal. Taking the island of Inchgarvie as their central point, they proposed to extend cantilevers from each side, which should meet similar cantilevers from the north and south shores, and thus form a continuous viaduct that would connect Fifeshire with West Lothian. The principle on which the cantilever is constructed is a very old one, but it has never been applied to the same extent or with the same materials as were used in this case.

The closing of the last opening between the cantilevers marks a great triumph for British engineering, and we may, therefore, profitably spend a short time in seeing how the bridge was built.

It may be well to show you first a view of the completed bridge whilst we explain the necessity which led to its construction.

A glance at the map of Scotland will show you that two great rivers, the Tay and Forth, run from west to east, and flow into the German Ocean. The North British Railway has had until now either to ferry goods and passengers across the Forth from Granton to Burntisland, and before the Tay Bridge was built, again at Dundee, or to take traffic round by Stirling.

To have an unbroken line it was necessary to bridge both Firths. Several suggestions for the Forth Bridge were considered, and at last it was decided to build a bridge on the suspension principle. Designs were accepted and Parliamentary sanction obtained, when the fall of the Tay Bridge gave a necessary warning to engineers on the point of strength and stability. The suspension principle was abandoned and the design prepared by Sir John Fowler and Mr. Benjamin Baker was adopted.

The points selected were North and South Queensferry. Here the river is about a mile in width, with the island of Inchgarvie lying about 1,700 feet from the north shore. The present view shows you the progress of the works as seen from above the approach viaduct.

General view of works

In speaking briefly as to how this great bridge was built, we will look first at the girder viaducts. These are built of stone, encased in granite, and although they look somewhat slim, are of considerable width. The building of these piers was an easy task compared to the rest of work. The method in which the girders were placed on the top was somewhat novel. They were built on a stage at the side of the piers and placed on the masonry when it was 18 feet high. Hydraulic jacks were placed underneath, by which the girder was raised bodily a foot at a time all the length of the viaduct.

The Approach Viaduct

As they had to be raised in this way 150 feet above high-water mark, it was a long and tedious operation but it did away with the expensive scaffolding commonly used. The first lift was made in April 1886, the last in July 1887. The girders are built of the best steel. The two cantilever piers, one on the Fife side and the other on the Queensferry shore, are of necessity much stronger than the others, though of similar construction. The dimensions of these piers are about 96 feet by 45 feet and they rise 209 feet above high-water mark, forming towers of great strength, to which are connected the main structures of the viaduct approaches.

A cantilever pier

The next part of the task was to construct the piers on which the three cantilevers were to rest.

A main pier

On the Queensferry side, the water is comparatively shallow, so the position was easily found. On the Fife side, the cantilever stands on the edge of the shore. The central cantilever is placed on Inchgarvie and had it not been for this little island, the bridge would probably have never been attempted. Inchgarvie is nothing more than a rock but on it stands a Norman Keep and a small battery, by means of which pirates were stopped when they chased vessels up the Forth.

To construct these piers, large circular caissons, 70 feet in diameter, were built. In shape they somewhat resemble gasometers. They were built on a cradle on shore, similar to that used in a shipbuilding yard. When empty they weighed about 400 tons but when filled with concrete, they weighed fully 15,000 tons. After being launched, they were towed out to their respective positions and sunk. The launching was attended with great ceremony, the caissons being decorated with flags, and many distinguished people being present. Our picture shows you one of these caissons after being launched. It is being towed out to its position.

A caisson being towed out

Let me, however, give you a nearer view of it before launching. This gives you a much better conception of its enormous size; the figures at the foot give you an idea of its height.

A caisson

Let us enter one of these caissons and see the arrangement. They have no bottom; but about 7 feet from the lower end there is an iron floor, the object of which was to make the space below resemble a diving bell. Entrance to this space was by means of double air-tight doors, so that workmen could descend into it and excavate the foundations for the piers. This chamber was lighted by electricity, and to ensure the safety of the men a pressure of about 2 atmospheres or 32 lbs on the square inch, was maintained by means of air pumps.

Caisson interior

On the top, as you will see from the picture, a temporary caisson or platform was erected, on which the mixing of the concrete and other work was conducted. Three shafts were constructed, the one to the right being for the men going up and down, the centre one for the concrete, and the left-hand one for other materials. The work in the lower part of the caisson had to be undertaken by a Parisian firm, as the home workmen were not accustomed to work under such high pressures of air. One of the caissons is no less than 90 feet under high-water mark. The caisson being filled to within a foot from the top with cement, the mason work was begun and carried up for 27 feet, the diameter being reduced to 50 feet. The material used is Arbroath stone bound with cement, and cased with Aberdeen granite. The total weight of the deepest pier is 20,000 tons.

The piers now being completed, let me, before speaking of the progress of the iron work, show you a picture giving the position of the three sets of piers known respectively as the Queensferry, Garvey, and Fife piers. You see here the distance to be bridged by the cantilevers, about which we will now try to give you a brief description.

Position of main piers

As soon as the piers were finished, the iron work was begun. From each pier rises a steel column, 12 feet in diameter. Into the mason work of the piers, 48 steel bolts, 2 1/2 inches in diameter had been sunk.

Four-inch solid steel plates, with a resisting power of 2,000 tons, were then riveted down, and to these were fastened the skewbacks. This is the term employed to indicate the junctions formed by the various parts of the cantilevers. It was therefore a matter of the greatest necessity that these should be of immense strength. Each skewback is the point where five steel tubes, three of which are 12 feet in diameter, and two 8 feet, meet. The four piers on which the cantilever rests are bound to each other by iron tubes.

A skewback

Let us now look at the vertical columns. They are 12 feet in diameter but vary in thickness as they rise. They are carried up to a height of 361 feet above sea level; if to this is added the 90 feet to which the lowest foundation was sunk, the result is a point that overtops St. Peter's in Rome and almost reaches as high as the Great Pyramid. This gives you a good idea of the magnitude of the work we are considering.

Vertical columns

These columns were built up bit by bit, just as a house is built, but instead of stone by stone, it was plate by plate. But how was the material raised? A temporary platform was built round the piers, and this was raised as required by hydraulic power. To secure the safety of the men working on the lower parts of the bridge from the falling of bolts, wire netting was placed at intervals. As the columns rise, they slope inwards, so that, although they are 120 feet at the base, at the top they are only 33 feet apart. As the four columns went up, the girders which held them in position grew with them.

This now leads us to speak of the cantilevers. If the work of building the columns was dangerous, that of constructing the cantilevers was much more so. In place of the large platform on which he worked, the workman was here suspended in mid-air. Like the columns, the projecting cantilevers were made by adding plate to plate, until the giant arms met.

Bottom member

Our picture shows what is called the lower or bottom member. The steel arm is 12 feet in diameter at the base; but after being carried upwards and outwards a distance of 680 feet, it has decreased to 5 feet. A movable platform was suspended round it and projected beyond the member about 10 feet. When a section was built, the rear part of the platform was unscrewed and placed in front, the crane was moved forward and another section added.

The upper member is built in much the same way as the lower, but it is a box lattice girder and not tubular. About the struts and ties we need not speak but will consider that the arms have been completed. We find that there is still a space of 350 feet to be bridged. This is done by means of immense girders, each weighing about 1,000 tons. One end of each girder is fastened to the cantilever but the other is not fixed, so that it can slide backwards and forwards as the bridge expands or contracts.

Upper member

The central girder connecting the south cantilever with Ingarvie was completed in October 1889 and the connections between the island erections and the Fife shore on November 7th.

Before passing on to show you some views of the completed bridge, it may interest some of you to see a photograph of an exceedingly clever and remarkable machine. It is the riveting machine invented by Mr. Arrol, one of the contractors. Usually the riveting had to be done by machines of simple form, worked by hydraulic power, but as the working space was small, direct-acting, hydraulic, four-inch cylinders were used. These compressed the rivet with a force equal to 3 tons per square inch.

There was no noise of hammering, but a silent pressure which made one end of the rivet as neat as the other. Previous to being put into the holes, the rivets were well heated in a furnace carried on the staging. Over eight million rivets, it is estimated, were used on the bridge.

A riveting machine

We will now show you one or two of the principal railway bridges in this Country. And first we will look at the new Tay Bridge, built by the same railway company, and we may naturally compare the two.

New Tay Bridge

The Tay Bridge is over two miles long, the Forth Bridge about one and a quarter miles. The Tay Bridge took five years to build, the Forth Bridge over seven. The weight of the iron and steel work of the Tay Bridge was 25,000 tons, that of the Forth Bridge is 54,000 tons, whilst there are 250,040 tons of solid masonry in the piers. Three million rivets hold the Tay Bridge together, it has taken eight million for the Forth Bridge. The Tay Bridge cost £650,000, the Forth Bridge will cost nearly £2,250,000.

We may next show a picture of the old Tay Bridge, which had such a sad history. It is almost certain that but for the accident at this Bridge, a bridge on the suspension principle would have been tried at South Queensferry.

Old Tay Bridge

The Britannia Tubular Bridge which spans the Menai Straits, ranks amongst the highest triumphs of engineering skill in modern times. Mr. Robert Stephenson was the engineer and the total cost was about £600,000. At each end of the bridge are two colossal lions (couchant) of Anglesey marble, weighing about eighty tons.

Britannia Tubular Bridge

Sunderland Bridge

The Sunderland Bridge is worthy of notice. It was opened in 1796. A stone bridge was proposed but was abandoned on the grounds of expense and the difficulty of obtaining proper foundations. The span is 236 feet, the height from low-water to the spring of the arch is about 60 feet. The cost was nearly £30,000, which has all been repaid by the foot toll, which was abolished in 1846. The bridge was almost entirely renewed in 1859 by the celebrated Robert Stephenson at a cost of £40,000 and remains to this day the largest single-arch, cast-iron bridge in England. The new railway bridge beside it is more useful than ornamental.

This diagram will give you an idea of the height of the Forth Bridge as compared with some of the principal buildings of the world.

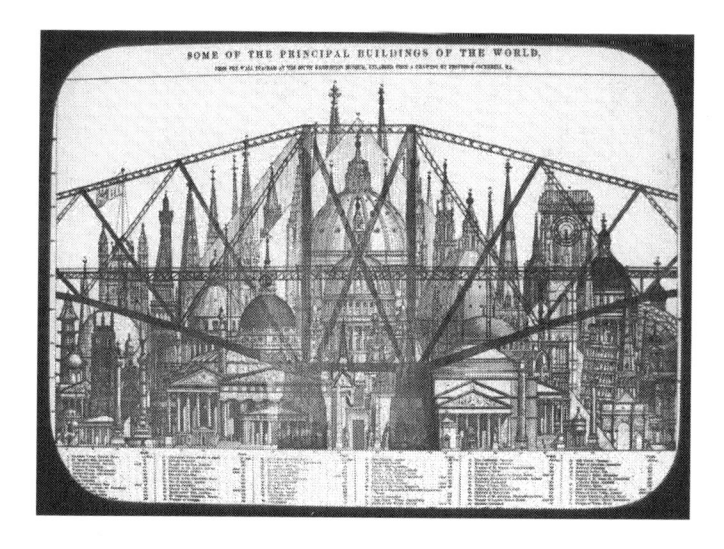

Comparative heights of other buildings

The highest spire, the one to the left, is Cologne Cathedral; the other is old St. Paul's, London. Next comes the Great Pyramid, which is only a few feet higher than the bridge we have been speaking about. St. Peter's at Rome and the Pyramid at Gheezah are about the same height.

We close with a very fine panorama. This picture is a direct photograph and gives you a capital idea of the magnitude of the Forth Bridge.

The George Washington Wilson Slides

In the series of lantern slides illustrating the formation of the Forth Bridge, the intention is to show, first, by means of skeleton sketches, the nature and qualities of the design and the foundations, and then, by photographs of the superstructure at different parts, and from various positions, to remark upon the progress made from time to time and the manner of building adopted, till finally we reach the completed viaduct, a view of which fitly completes the selection.

Longitudinal Section

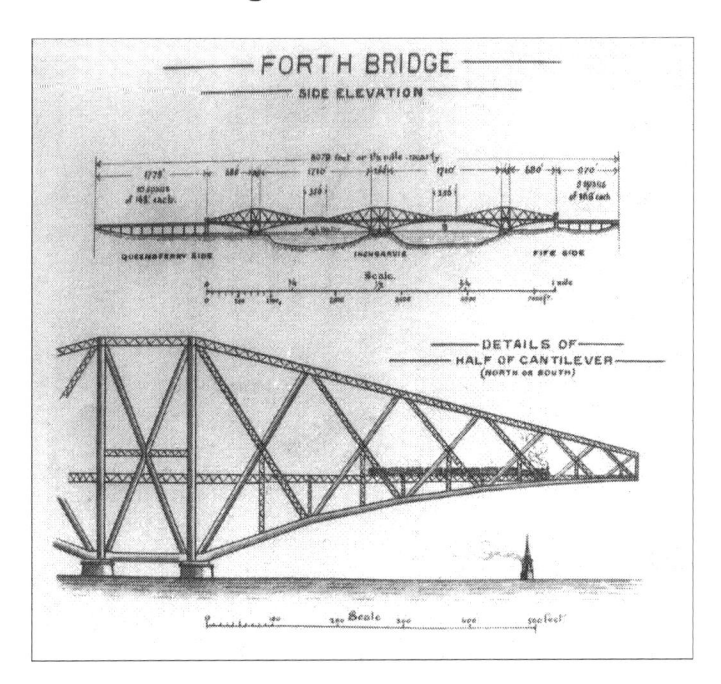

The decision to build a bridge connecting Edinburgh directly with the North, has been the result of the keen competition between the two leading Scottish railways along with their several allies, the English Trunk lines.

This is by no means a new idea however, for, at the beginning of this century, a company was attempted to be floated in Edinburgh to build a viaduct on the exact site of the present gigantic structure. The chances for the company being a paying one may be imagined when it is stated that the capital of the company was to be £150,000, whereas the present bridge, constructed with the aid of the best and latest inventions in material and labour-saving tools, has cost, with approaches, from first to last, some £3,500,000, 'though the estimated cost before starting was less by £1,850,000.

The Forth being exceedingly deep, it was resolved to bridge it at Queensferry, opposite the island of Inchgarvie, so as to take advantage of it for the foundations of the central pier. The depth of water in the divisions of the Forth on each side (200 feet) made it necessary that the adjacent piers should be close to the land on each bank; and, as the Board of Trade stipulated that the shipping plying up and down the estuary should be in no way hampered, the spans had to provide sufficient headway to permit the tallest-masted vessel afloat to pass through. The height fixed on, 150 feet clear of the water, amply allows for this, while two giant strides, of

1,710 feet each, from Inchgarvie to the Fife and Midlothian sides, made it possible to found the side cantilevers in comparatively shallow water.

Tableau of Principle

The span and the height of the bridge above the water being settled, the engineers had to select a principle for its design and decided that a cantilever bridge would best suit the requirements. The word is novel to the uninitiated, as applied to bridge construction, but the principle has been frequently applied, and was known to be used by the Chinese, probably for ages. The disposition of the strains in a cantilever, like those of the Forth Bridge, may be roughly shown in the accompanying tableau-vivant.

It will be seen that the arms are in tension, acting as ties, and that each rod is in compression and acts as a strut. At the same time, it will be evident that each individual is (provided he be equally weighted at both extremities) totally independent of his neighbours, which explains how it was possible to erect each cantilever without any support from the others or from below, and in such a top-heavy looking manner. No doubt, the extreme difficulty of erecting supporting scaffolding in so impracticable a situation, and the advantage of leaving the channel unobstructed during the erection of the bridge, greatly influenced the engineers in their choice of design.

Cross Section at Pier

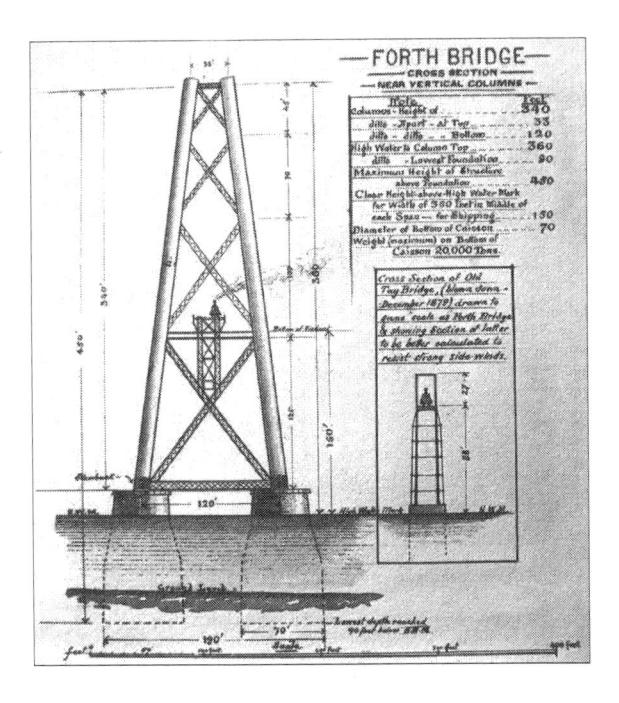

This shows a cross-section at one of the three central piers. The three piers are all similar in cross-section but the middle (or Inchgarvie) pier is wider measuring *along* the bridge; the two outer piers being 145 feet each along the bridge, while the centre pier is 260 feet.

The width of the piers *across* the bridge, as shown on the screen, is, at the base, 120 feet, and narrows to 33 feet at the top. The height of the steelwork is 333 feet or 360 feet above the high-water mark of ordinary spring tides; and, as the deepest caisson reaches down to 90 feet below that, the maximum height, measured from the foundations, is 450 feet. The decrease in width as the height increases, is considerable, and is intended to enable the fabric to better withstand lateral wind pressure. This power of inertia is increased by enlarging the base as compared with the area of the superstructure; a factory chimney and one of the Egyptian pyramids being good examples of buildings of the least-suited and the best-suited forms of construction for weathering every gale.

That mistakes have been made in planning bridges in similar exposed situations by not reckoning sufficiently with this sometimes immense force, will be understood by all who remember the disastrous end of the first Tay Bridge, which was blown down in December, 1879. For comparison with the present Forth Bridge, the skeleton cross-section of the ill-fated Tay Bridge is shown drawn to the same scale. It will be seen that the Forth Bridge, with its legs well parted at the feet, has a much more stable appearance than the upright columns of Tay Bridge, and the designers affirm that each pier, although it has to stand the pressure of the wind on a length of about one third of a mile of superstructure, will safely bear a cyclonic pressure of 56 lbs per square inch blowing *eastward* on one of its cantilever arms and simultaneously, *westwood* on the other. Such a test it is never likely to undergo, as these conditions are far more severe than anything recorded in our Country; for, during the storm of unprecedented severity to which the old Tay Bridge succumbed, the highest pressure reached was estimated by experts at 30 lbs per square inch.

Skeleton Plan, showing taper

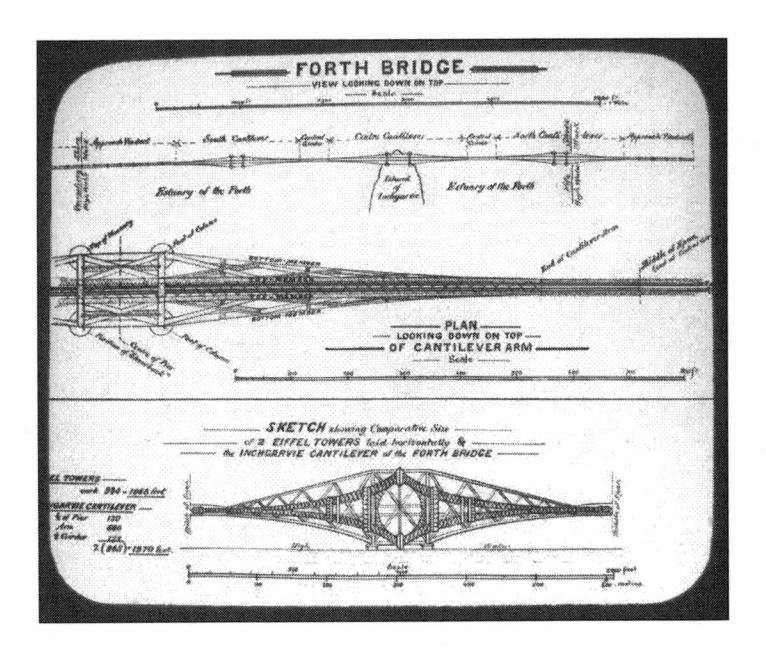

As may be seen on this plan, the cantilevers taper, not only from the base to the top of the piers but also from the base of the pier to the outer end of the lower member of each cantilever arm, and in a much less degree to the extremities of the top members. As the strains on the several sections of the cantilever arms decrease in intensity as we get further from the piers, so the girders and tubes are made proportionately lighter, to economise material and ensure that, as nearly as possible, all the ironwork shall be equally effective.

In the two centre spans, the ends of the cantilevers are connected by lattice girders 350 feet long and weighing 800 tons each. The railway runs between and level with the bottom of these girders, which are fastened at one end only in order to allow of expansion and contraction from change of temperature. The total change of length provided for on the bridge is seven feet, or at the rate of one inch in every hundred feet.

Caissons Floating Out

FORTH BRIDGE
Sketch showing a Caisson
floating in Position
for Loading and Sinking

The foundations for the three cantilever fabrics are three sets or clusters of four columns each. These columns are formed of a lower iron tube or caisson, which is sunk into the ground and then filled with concrete, and above the caisson, on the top of the concrete, masonry is built 27 feet high, to bring the height up to the level from which the lower boom of the cantilever springs.

These caissons were made in Glasgow and fitted together in the Bridge Works at Queensferry; when empty, each weighed about 400 tons, and when filled with concrete should weigh about 15,000 tons. The caisson consists of a tube within a tube, the outer one being 70 feet diameter at the bottom and 60 feet diameter at the top. Seven feet from the lower cutting edge, an air-tight floor was built, beneath which, when sunk in position, excavation was carried on.

The launching of these caissons was sometimes attended by a good deal of ceremonial and was held as a general holiday by the workmen and local inhabitants generally. Many distinguished visitors took part in the proceedings on these auspicious occasions, and, in the usual manner, broke a bottle of wine for luck, by throwing it against the side of the tub-like vessel as it 'took the water'.

The caisson having been safely launched, was towed out to its ultimate destination, where (after having had a temporary additional ring of plates fastened onto the top of the caisson, to keep out the water at high tide) 2,000 tons of concrete were filled in, causing the whole gasometer-like mass to settle down in the position chosen for it. An accident, which caused great delay, happened to one of the caissons while floating near its position, for, after being towed out, at low-water it stuck in the mud so fast that the lifting tendency of the returning tide was insufficient to float it before the water rose to the level of the upper edge of the caisson, which then, of course, quickly became filled, and lost all further inclination to even attempt to float until after nine months of labour and ingenuity; when, by transforming the submerged caisson into a watertight barrel, and pumping it dry, it resumed the *status quo* once more.

Queensferry Foundations

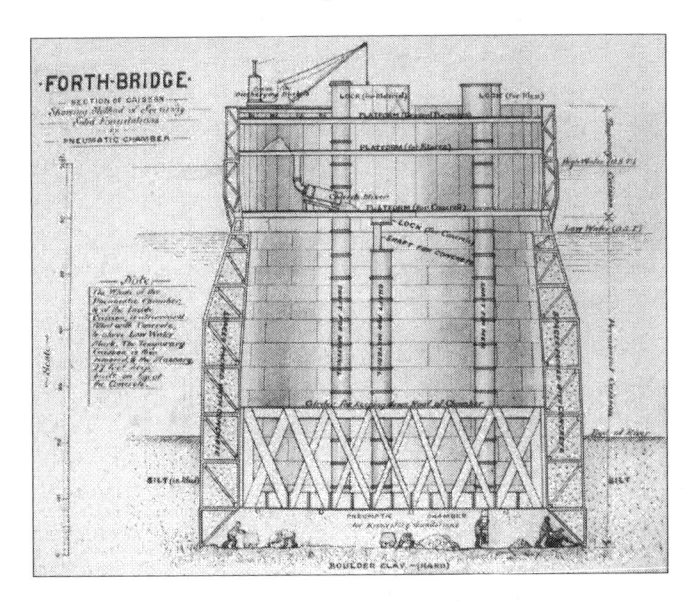

On the top of the permanent caisson, a platform was laid for mixing concrete and on the top of the temporary portion a platform was provided for general purposes. As has already been mentioned, each caisson was provided with an iron floor seven feet from the bottom. This airtight diaphragm served to divide it into two separate chambers, the lower of which was, when in the water, simply a huge diving bell, and the men who entered it to dig the foundations did so through a vertical shaft with an air-tight lock at the top. The air pumped into them under pressure, as will be explained afterwards, drove the water down in the chamber, and enabled them to breath. The materials excavated and concrete were passed in and out through traps working on a similar principle.

As for every 32 feet that we descend below water level we require an additional pressure of 15 lbs to the square inch, to force the water down to that level, it will be apparent that before the maximum depth attained was reached, the workmen in their underground cell, were labouring under very great disadvantages. The pressure occasionally reached as high as 48 lbs per square inch when the bed of the river had an unusual depth of thin mud; afterwards, as firmer strata were touched by the lower or cutting edge of the caisson, it became possible to considerably reduce this air pressure.

For this submarine work, men had to be specially brought from Belgium, where large dock constructions have necessitated the training of great numbers of men to toil under similar conditions. During excavation, the interior of the excavated chamber was lit by electricity, and the labour was greatly facilitated by Mr. Arrol's invention of a special mechanical digger, worked by hydraulic power. The chamber was occupied on average by about thirty workmen at a time and many visitors went through the disagreeable experience of swallowing compressed air and descending the shaft to the mine below.

An amusing anecdote is related of a gentleman who carried a flask of spirits down with him and broached it before ascending again. It took him so long to get to the top of the ladder that, when in the air-tight chamber, he produced the pocket pistol once more, but on stepping into the open air it burst like a hand-grenade, to his great consternation, the reason being, of course, that the pressure outside the bottle was insufficient to counteract the compressed air that he had admitted.

When the caisson had reached its proper depth in the boulder clay, the air chamber was filled with concrete, well packed, as was also the upper body of the caisson. An addition of stonework, 27 feet high, brought the column up to the level for laying the steel plate for carrying the bridge. This plate was fastened down by 48 steel bolts, each two and a half inches in diameter, and piercing the stonework from top to bottom.

Difficulty was experienced in keeping the caisson upright in several cases where the foundations were on a sloping rocky bottom, as it became necessary that the outer edge should be temporarily supported on heaps of sandbags and banks of concrete placed by divers. The rock being gradually blasted away by dynamite, the temporary supports were lowered and adjusted as the caisson sank and secured for itself a solid and level rock foundation. It is computed that the greatest weight on the bottom of one of the caissons will not exceed five and a half tons per square foot.

Upright Part of Cantilever

On top of the masonry, two steel bed-plates are fastened by means of the 24 bolts already referred to. The lower plate weighs 40 tons and is rigidly attached. The holes in the upper steel bed-plate, through which pass the tops of the huge bolts, are not circular but oval. This allows the whole super incumbent mass to move bodily to the extent of a few inches in a direction across the river when expansion from heat occurs. In the case of wind, the heads of the bolts would prevent any tendency to rising, so that, paradoxically, because the bridge is not secured but allowed freely to accommodate itself, it is more secure than if it had been rigidly attached to the piers.

The various tubes and girders that spring from each pier are all attached to a sort of compound socket or joint known as a skewback, the base of which is the upper bed-plate already mentioned. The skewback is, as it were, the focus at which the principal thrusts in the bridge converge. It is situated nearly in the centre of the pier, and its complicated construction may be surmised when it is known that from it spring five girders and five tubes, three of the latter being 12 feet in diameter and two 8 feet.

Each upright column, 340 feet high, is 12 feet in diameter throughout, and is built of steel plates, gradually diminishing in thickness to the top. The outside shell of the tubes and columns is connected transversely in the interior by a network of braces.

The outside plates were bent and fitted and the rivet holes drilled, in the works on shore, and were then, one by one, riveted together on the pier in their respective places. The riveting was all done by hydraulic power and unattended by noise, so that the impression conveyed was that the fabric was, as it were, growing, from day-to-day, each addition being entirely unheralded by the usual din of the boilermaker's hammer.

The gradual heightening of the columns by the addition of plates was done from a platform which was supported by lifting-girders projecting through, and fastened to, the part already executed, and they were raised as required, also by hydraulic power. The necessary riveting was performed in a circular cage surrounded by wire netting, attached by iron straps to the lifting-girders just mentioned. Although the columns are vertical when seen from up and down the river, they converge from 120 feet apart at the base to 33 feet at the top when seen from either end of the bridge, for reasons connected with the stability of the structure, as has already been explained.

From the top of these columns on a clear day, a beautiful view is obtained for many miles in every direction. The hydraulic lifts used for raising the workmen and materials were, during the period of construction, available to make the ascent easy for privileged sightseers. A strong staircase, which zigzags up the diagonal bracing to the top, may still be ascended by those of an energetic disposition, as it formally was by many who placed not their faith in hydraulic lifts.

Mode of Building Out Cantilever

In the cantilever arms, the bottom members are the tubes that spring outward from the skewback and although the general impression conveyed by them is that of a curved arch, closer inspection shows that each of the six lengths of which they are composed is perfectly straight, and is of gradually smaller diameter as the outer end of each arm is approached; for example, the first length begins at 12 feet diameter, the next at 10 feet 6 inches, and so on, so that the real shape is something like a long telescope drawn out and slightly bent at the end of each joint. The total projection of the points of these bottom members is 680 feet from the centre of the skewback, where they are 120 feet apart, and at the point where they approach to within 22 feet of each other.

The top members are the girders which, having connected the two vertical columns at the top, slant downward and outward to the extremity of the arm, and at the same time converge slightly, viz., from 33 to 22 feet apart. Like the bottom members, these girders gradually decrease in section as they recede from the pier, and as they are therefore built on what may be called a compound slant, as well as tapering, the difficulties to be overcome in fitting them and their connections together can hardly be realised by anyone who has not been engaged in such work.

There are six tubular struts to each bottom member, each decreasing in calibre and length, and increasing in slant or rake as they approach the centre of the span. The length of the shortest is 75 feet, that of the longest 340 feet. In section, they are like a circle with flattened sides, the flat parts being utilised to effect junctions with the girders that are fastened to them.

The six ties which descend from each top member are attached to the bottom member at each point where the corresponding next strut slants upward from it, these junctions being formed by modified skewbacks. As each pair of ties and struts crosses approximately at their centres and traverses the same distance horizontally, they form, when viewed from the side, a series of diamond-shaped openings, gradually decreasing in size and varied in shape, which tends to break that monotony of angle which is so noticeable and disagreeable to the eye in very many iron bridges and structures. The ties, like the top members, consist of rectangular lattice girders, and are of lighter construction as they get shorter.

To further support the great weight of tube in the lower member, it is held up by a vertical tie connecting it at the centre of each bay with the intersection of the tie and strut overhead. These vertical ties also support the viaduct girders, which thread their way through the network of steel, each girder diminishing in depth as the distance between its supports becomes less.

Progress of Work

The view projected on screen shows the undertaking as it appeared in May 1889, about six and a half years after first breaking ground, and within measurable distance of the grand consummation. An idea of the vast size of the work, both in its detail and as a whole, may be tolerably grasped by observing the insect-like appearance presented by one or two of the men, to whose fearless and patient toil we owe the up-rearing of this latest Wonder of the World.

The method of extending the several limbs of the bridge can be seen by noticing the platform at the outer extremities of each unfinished tube girder. Each is supplied with steam crane and also with hydraulic riveters and rivet heating furnaces. The method pursued is as follows:

full-sized drawings are made of each separate plate and bar in the drawing office, and the steel being adjusted exactly to these in the works, is then, also in the works, accurately fitted together, the rivet holes bored and each part marked, taken apart and stored 'til required. It is then conveyed out along the pier constructed at Queensferry, or out in boats, to beneath the position it is to occupy.

The steam-crane tackle hoists it to the platform where it is refitted together, and the requisite rivets heated, and, one by one, inserted in the holes bored for them, when the two arms of the hydraulic riveter, placed opposite each end of the rivets, close in a silent but resistless embrace, which moulds the flat point of the rivet into a semi-circular head.

At first, a good many accidents were caused by rivets being allowed to drop from aerial platforms, as, by the time they reached the water level or lower staging, their velocity resembled that of a bullet but, afterwards, this was prevented by hanging wire netting immediately beneath these platforms to intercept them. In all, about six million rivets were used, and those whose talents lie in that direction have made curious calculations as, for example, that they would reach, when placed end to end, a length of 380 miles.

Frequently in building out long girders and tubes in advance of the rest of the structure, temporary supporting girders, cables or chains had to be attached, to keep their progress in correct line, until they reached the next point of support. When finished, these cantilever arms are (Mr. Baker, one of the designers affirms), strong enough to support six of the largest ironclads suspended from their extremities.

End of Shore Cantilever

It will be noticed that the two arms of the central cantilever are equally weighted, each having to support one half the burden of the central girder extending from it, but apparently those on the Fife and Queensferry cantilevers, while built almost symmetrically, are not in an equally balanced state, for they have no girders or half-girders to keep down the shore ends. The absence of this is compensated for, and equilibrium re-established, by making these outside arms ten feet longer and, in addition, by holding them down by means of huge bolts built into the masonry, so contrived as to admit of the sliding movement caused by the contraction and expansion of the bridge, but resisting vertical movement as they are anchored down to a mass weighing 1,000 tons.

Provision has had to be made at the extremity of each cantilever arm for the safe adjustment of the rails, when, owing to expansion caused by a great rise in temperature, the ends of two adjacent arms have moved nearer to each other by say one foot. To lay rails in the ordinary manner at these points, where the whole expansion due to one arch is concentrated, would only bring about consequences similar to what took place in the first railways, when the science of rail laying was not understood. At that time, the rails were laid butting close against each other, with the result that, on a warm day, as there was no provision made for expansion longitudinally, the rails were forced up into a series of arches, with their chairs and sleepers hanging to them. In the Forth Bridge, the expansion is allowed for, at the point named, by making the joints on a long slant, each end forming a pointed wedge which is pushed by elongation passed the other point, so that the fact of these taper-pointed rails projecting a few inches more or less passed each other will make no difference to the continuity of the rails or their fitness to allow of railway traffic being conducted smoothly over them.

Approach Viaducts

The interest and novelty of the Forth Bridge undoubtedly centres in the three great cantilevers, but the approach viaducts at each end are also considerable undertakings and no account of the bridge would be complete without mention being made of them.

The approach viaduct on the Fife side has five spans, while that at Queensferry has ten. These spans are each 168 feet from centre to centre of the piers, and the girders, which are of steel, and 22 feet 6 inches in depth, are of the ordinary lattice-bar type. The peculiarity in the method of their erection lies in this, that the masonry piers were not *first* erected (entailing difficulty in transporting building material), and the girders *afterwards* built across them (which, as they are about 130 feet above water level, would have necessitated complex and expensive scaffolding), but, the girders were built on the piers as soon as these were raised a sufficient height above the ground to admit it; and hydraulic power, so many applications of which have been used in constructing the bridge, was taken advantage of to raise the girders above the stonework, so as to allow additional courses of masonry to be laid, and the operation repeated 'til the full height was attained.

Inside the girders, a temporary floor and tramway was laid, along which were run the wagons in which the granite blocks for the piers arrived, depositing their load at several points, as required, the wagons having first been hoisted by steam power to the level reached by the girder.

Considering the amount of work to be accomplished, the time occupied in building these stone piers, from first to last, namely fifteen months, must be allowed to have been very short. The lifting of the girders by the hydraulic jacks occupied, at first, almost a day, but, as experience developed and better methods were applied, this time was shortened to a period of less than four hours, even when a row of ten spans was to be elevated simultaneously.

Beyond what has been remarked, there is no special peculiarity about these approach viaducts lest it be their exceptional height and the remarkable dimensions of the terminal piers. At the foundations, these measure 100 feet by 50 feet and the same size is maintained up till 18 feet above high water, from which point they begin again at 70 feet by 40 feet and diminish to 50 feet by 25 feet at rail-level, above which they rise 50 feet. All the piers were of Aberdeen granite outside and of sandstone within.

Bridge Completed

Connection from end to end of the viaduct was achieved in October 1889, almost seven years after the undertaking was commenced, and 'through' passengers for the North from England can now, by availing themselves of it and the new Tay Bridge, reach Perth and the North country one hour sooner than they formally could. Besides the advantage in mileage gained by erecting the Forth Bridge, the fact that it may be considered the greatest engineering marvel of the age will tend to draw passengers toward it in preference to the longer opposition route.

One would expect that the traffic would need to be large to justify the expense of such Leviathan bridges as those at Queensferry and Dundee; and that it is, at certain seasons, immense, and well worth competing for, anyone can realise who witnesses the commotion in one of the great London railway termini or at Perth Station during the first half of August when, besides the crowds of tourists, holiday seekers, and businessmen, the great annual migration northward of sportsmen, with their followers, horses and dogs, takes place.

The following figures relating to the bridge are rather interesting. The quantity of Siemens-Martin steel used was 54,000 tons; of cement, 20,000 tons; of granite, 707,000 cubic feet; of masonry and concrete, 117,000 cubic yards; and of timber, 1,000,000 cubic feet, chiefly used in constructing the jetty and preparatory works. The surface of steel which will have to be painted measures 20 acres fully. The number of men employed was at times as many as 5,000 and the deaths caused by accident averaged about one every six weeks since the work was begun, the total amounting to fifty six, which, 'though it seems high, cannot be wondered at considering the extremely hazardous nature of the work.

Comparisons, though they may be odious, will inevitably be made in discussing the Forth Bridge. As regards the length of the spans, it is easily first with 1,710 feet, being well seconded by the Brooklyn Bridge at New York with 1,600; the latter is, however, a suspension bridge. It is easily beaten in total length by, for example, its next-door neighbour the Tay Bridge, which is two and a quarter miles long and three quarters of a mile longer than the Forth Bridge. It is by far the highest bridge in the world and, indeed, only three buildings of any kind over-top it, viz., the spire of Cologne Cathedral, the Great Pyramid of Egypt and the Eiffel Tower in Paris. The last mentioned is, however, not to be compared in audacity of conception, difficulty of execution, scientific interest or practical utility to the Forth Bridge, which holds in rigid extension between each pair of Herculean shoulders a length of steelwork nearly twice as long as the Eiffel Tower is high and which, while delicately adjusted to allow of adaptation to the slightest change in the dimensions of its parts, is at the same time of strength so immense, that the weight of a couple of ponderous mineral trains passing along it at a distance of 850 feet from the nearest point of support, can be treated as a matter of little moment, it being but a trifle compared with the ever-present strain necessary to maintain its own colossal form and stand immovable under the furious attack of a hurricane.

Having now described the work and workmanship of the Forth Bridge, it only remains to name the masterminds who planned and directed it.

The designers were Sir (then Mr.) John Fowler and Sir (then Mr.) Benjamin Baker, the well-known civil engineers. The contractors or builders were Messrs. Tancred, Arrol and Co. Ltd. and it is only justice to say that it is in great measure owing to the many inventions of special methods and tools by Sir (then Mr.) William Arrol during the progress of work, and, in general, the extraordinary resource displayed by him, that the task has so well and, in so short a time, been successfully completed. The ingenious theory of 1882, formulated in the fertile brain of the scientific designer, has, in 1889, resulted, at the hands of the skilled craftsmen, the present gigantic fact - the Forth Bridge - which stands an enduring monument to the genius that conceived it, to the faith and enterprise that promoted it and the perseverance, skill, and daring that have, at last, brought it to a successful issue ..... a veritable triumph of the Iron Age.

Andrew Gill: I have collected historical photographs and optical antiques for over forty years. I am a professional 'magic lantern' showman presenting Victorian slide shows and giving talks on early optical entertainments for museums, festivals, special interest groups and universities. Please visit my website **'Magic Lantern World'** at www.magiclanternist.com

My booklets and photo albums are available from Amazon, simply search for the titles below. If you've enjoyed this book, please leave a review on Amazon, as good ratings are very important to independent authors. If you're disappointed, please let me know the reason, so that I can address the issue in future editions.

Historical travel guides
New York
Jersey in 1921
Norwich in 1880
Doon the Watter
Liverpool in 1886
Nottingham in 1899
Bournemouth in 1914
Great Yarmouth in 1880
Victorian Walks in Surrey
The Way We Were: Bath
A Victorian Visit to Brighton
The Way We Were: Lincoln
A Victorian Visit to Hastings
A Victorian Visit to Falmouth
Newcastle upon Tyne in 1903
Victorian and Edwardian York
The Way We Were: Llandudno
A Victorian Visit to North Devon
The Way We Were: Manchester
A Victorian Guide to Birmingham
Leeds through the Magic Lantern

An Edwardian Guide to Leicester
Victorian and Edwardian Bradford
Victorian and Edwardian Sheffield
The Way We Were: North Cornwall
A Victorian Visit to Fowey and Looe
A Victorian Visit to Peel, Isle of Man
Doncaster through the Magic Lantern
The Way We Were: The Lake District
Lechlade to Oxford by Canoe in 1875
Guernsey, Sark and Alderney in 1921
East Devon through the Magic Lantern
The River Thames from Source to Sea
A Victorian Visit to Ramsey, Isle of Man
A Victorian Visit to Douglas, Isle of Man
Victorian Totnes through the Magic Lantern
Victorian Whitby through the Magic Lantern
Victorian London through the Magic Lantern
St. Ives through the Victorian Magic Lantern
Victorian Torquay through the Magic Lantern
Victorian Glasgow through the Magic Lantern
The Way We Were: Wakefield and Dewsbury
The Way We Were: Hebden Bridge to Halifax
Victorian Blackpool through the Magic Lantern
Victorian Scarborough through the Magic Lantern
The Way We Were: Hull and the Surrounding Area
The Way We Were: Harrogate and Knaresborough
A Victorian Tour of North Wales: Rhyl to Llandudno
A Victorian Visit to Lewes and the surrounding area
The Isle of Man through the Victorian Magic Lantern
A Victorian Visit to Helston and the Lizard Peninsula
A Victorian Railway Journey from Plymouth to Padstow
A Victorian Visit to Barmouth and the Surrounding Area
The Way We Were: Holmfirth, Honley and Huddersfield
A Victorian Visit to Malton, Pickering and Castle Howard
A Victorian Visit to Eastbourne and the surrounding area
A Victorian Visit to Aberystwyth and the Surrounding Area
The Way We Were: Rotherham and the Surrounding Area
A Victorian Visit to Castletown, Port St. Mary and Port Erin
Penzance and Newlyn through the Victorian Magic Lantern
A Victorian Journey to Snowdonia, Caernarfon and Pwllheli
Victorian Brixham and Dartmouth through the Magic Lantern
Victorian Plymouth and Devonport through the Magic Lantern
A Victorian Tour of North Wales: Conwy to Caernarfon via Anglesey
Staithes, Runswick and Robin Hood's Bay through the Magic Lantern
Dawlish, Teignmouth and Newton Abbot through the Victorian Magic Lantern

Walking Books
Victorian Edinburgh Walks
Victorian Rossendale Walks
More Victorian Rossendale Walks
Victorian Walks on the Isle of Wight (Book 1)
Victorian Walks on the Isle of Wight (Book 2)
Victorian Rossendale Walks: The End of an Era

Other historical topics
The YMCA in the First World War
Sarah Jane's Victorian Tour of Scotland
The River Tyne through the Magic Lantern
The 1907 Wrench Cinematograph Catalogue
Victorian Street Life through the Magic Lantern
The First World War through the Magic Lantern
Ballyclare May Fair through the Victorian Magic Lantern
The Story of Burnley's Trams through the Magic Lantern
The Franco-British 'White City' London Exhibition of 1908
The 1907 Wrench 'Optical and Science Lanterns' Catalogue
The CWS Crumpsall Biscuit Factory through the Magic Lantern
How They Built the Forth Railway Bridge: A Victorian Magic Lantern Show

Historical photo albums (just photos)
The Way We Were: Suffolk
Norwich: The Way We Were
The Way We Were: Somerset
Fife through the Magic Lantern
York through the Magic Lantern
Rossendale: The Way We Were
The Way We Were: Cumberland
Burnley through the Magic Lantern
Oban to the Hebrides and St. Kilda
Tasmania through the Magic Lantern
Swaledale through the Magic Lantern
Llandudno through the Magic Lantern
Birmingham through the Magic Lantern
Penzance, Newlyn and the Isles of Scilly
Great Yarmouth through the Magic Lantern
Ancient Baalbec through the Magic Lantern
The Isle of Skye through the Magic Lantern
Ancient Palmyra through the Magic Lantern
The Kentish Coast from Whitstable to Hythe
New South Wales through the Magic Lantern
From Glasgow to Rothesay by Paddle Steamer
Victorian Childhood through the Magic Lantern
The Way We Were: Yorkshire Railway Stations
Southampton, Portsmouth and the Great Liners

Newcastle upon Tyne through the Magic Lantern
Egypt's Ancient Monuments through the Magic Lantern
The Way We Were: Birkenhead, Port Sunlight and the Wirral
Ancient Egypt, Baalbec and Palmyra through the Magic Lantern

Copyright © 2021 by Andrew Gill. All rights reserved. No part of this book may be reproduced or used in any manner without written permission of the copyright owner.

Contact email: victorianhistory@virginmedia.com

Made in the USA
Coppell, TX
20 March 2023